WASH DAY

USING ELECTRICITY

Series Editor, Nick Montfort

Using Electricity is a series of computer generated books, meant to actually reward reading in conventional and unconventional ways. The series title takes a line from the computer generated poem "A House of Dust," developed by Alison Knowles with James Tenney in 1967. This work, a FORTRAN computer program and a significant early generator of poetic text, combines different lines to produce descriptions of houses.

Nick Montfort, *The Truelist*

Rafael Pérez Y Pérez, *Mexica: 20 Years—20 Stories* [*Mexica: 20 años—20 historias*]

Allison Parrish, *Articulations*

Ranjit Bhatnagar, *Encomials: Sonnets from Pentametron*

Li Zilles, *Machine, Unlearning*

Milton Läufer, *A Noise Such as a Man Might Make*

Stephanie Strickland, *Ringing the Changes*

Jörg Piringer, *Data Poetry*

Hannes Bajohr, *Blanks*

Rena J. Mosteirin, *Experiment 116*

John Cayley, *Image Generation*

Arwa Michelle Mboya, *Wash Day*

Qianxun Chen and Mariana Roa Oliva, *Seedlings_: Walk in Time*

ARWA MICHELLE MBOYA

WASH DAY

Counterpath
DENVER AND NEW YORK
2023

Counterpath
counterpathpress.org

Library of Congress Control Number 2022059493

ISBN 978-1-93-399681-3 (paperback)

CONTENTS

PROLOGUE

welcome to my channel

i hate it here
what's up you guys my name is ___ and today i'm back with another
video already -

[...]

hello everyone welcome back to my
channel oh my god i love to have you
here if you're new here hey
what's up how's it going if you're
coming back here for yet another video i
love to have you here -

[...]

with this terrible awful year
can we can we leave that can we not
bring that can that be cancelled since
y'all will cancel everything
can we cancel that can we cancel the
___ typing system
all together because because i just
don't get the purpose of labeling
our ___ because they really don't do
nothing like it does nothing for your

[...]

hey guys
welcome to my channel it's me
to ___ out of my
___ so i want to mainly
focus on my ___
because once i -

[...]

welcome to my channel my
name is lex legs of my
___ i just went in with
my my ___ enhancing smoothie

[...]

hey guys welcome back to my channel today i do
today was a routine so i promise you guys in
each section to my ___ dried up
so i'm just gonna go ahead and measure that -

___
which leads me into my next
unpopular opinion a person's ___
pattern
does not mean anything when it comes to
your ___ people are fixated on that
typing system to the point where
they will follow somebody
based off the typing system you know
because they look at ___ and it looks like their ___ so they're
like seeing you know and i get it you're
seeing a reflection of you like this is

my ___ type i'm looking at my ___ type
and believe in my head because this is
the ___ type that i'm watching
that i'm going to get the same results
as them like this is what people
do and that's not right
like because you're sit up here so
fixated on
___ typing that you sit up here and
forget the things that are really
important
because ___ type which is the way your

[...]

hey everyone
where you welcome video
to here to ___ my ___
do you feel the dry of
my ___ and it looks so
healthy but once again -

[...]

hey guys welcome back to my channel okay
we have another natural ___ video
so today i'm going to be showing you how
i get my ___
from this to this yes so i'm going to be
showing you my full ___ routine
my ___ routine and a little ___ tutorial so-

[...]

hey beauties what going on welcome back
to my channel let's get into this a ___
because this ___ just looking too
musty and crusty

[...]

oh my god i love
to have you here thank
you for joining me again
so today we are going to
be doing a ___ so
i applied that all in my-

[...]

-is that i'm not gonna follow people that
look just like me in their ___
mind you ___ is beautiful right but i
like diversity i
i don't care really what your ___ pattern is
i want to know about these
products
and i want to know about okay that's
your low density but i like
the ___ and i want to watch the
review of that particular person's
___ and i'm gonna probably watch a
couple other ones

[...]

welcome to my channel
to~~day i am bringing to~~

you a ___ routine and
honestly it looks down
in the middle of my head
i decided to do my
favorite ___: the ___
and go i applied the
white peony ___ i thought it
was this whole time i
thought it was a regular
___ i think i
like do a bit of damage
but because i do not
find that it flakes act
also i can have my ___ -

[...]

hey guys welcome back to my channel it's
just a little bit more of a true
thing about this year when i ___
my ___ because it was like mine that
my ___ is so thick it would like to
subscribe if you haven't already

[...]

but i'm not sitting up here because this
person has
___ ___ ___ that mean i'm not
going to watch them
why that's stupid that don't even make
any sense
because at the end of the day my ___ is
my ___ my ___ are my strengths so
even if we got similarities
with our ___ don't mean nothing that

doesn't mean a damn thing to me
my ___ is still going to come looking
like my ___ because we are
all unique and we're all different -

[...]

welcome back to my channel as you can
see from the title we are going to be
doing my winter ___ routine so this
routine is the most moisturizing I
promise you it gets my ___ from like
crusty to just moisturize and bouncy and
this can last up to two weeks untouched
I am not even playing with you guys if -

[...]

hey y'all welcome back to my channel it
is ___ here back with another video
and today i'm going to be walking you
guys through my ___ routine
this was a highly requested video on my
instagram if you don't follow me on
instagram you definitely -

[...]

welcome back to my channel
welcome to my channel if you're new here
my name is ___ and yes
___ is my real surname
so today's video is in sponsorship with
___ they are an amazing brand
they are the first ever revolutionary
brand dedicated

to specifically ___ types
yes you heard me right this is a
black-owned business that is
specifically made
for people with ___ the best part is
these products are made by women with ___

[...]

hey guys welcome back to my channel
today i am bringing to you a ___
routine and
also some information about how i ___
my___
so i also will be talking about some
information about how i ___ my ___ how
many times i ___ my ___
what i use in the ___ type of ___ i
use the fallout i get
um all that stuff i'm going to be giving
you all i have
on my ___ day so i hope you enjoy also
today's video is sponsored by ___
one of my favorite brands which is a
customizable ___ and ___

[...]

hey guys what's up its ___ here
welcome back to my channel thank you for
clicking on this video if you're new
make sure you hit the subscribe button -

[...]

hello everyone and welcome to my channel

my name is ___ and welcome back
to another video so in today's video
I'll be showing you how I define this
kinky ___ from a twigs without
using ___ if you're a regular on my
channel you know that I really love
wearing kinky ___ and it can get
quite expensive using ___ all the time
to define the ___ and we all know that
___ isn't always the best option whether
you're using ___ or your own ___
so I was sent over this ___ by a
company called ___ and I have four
___ of kinky ___ I also
got a complimentary ___ and a
___ now the reason why I only got
four ___ and not more is because-

[...]

hey guys thanks for clicking on this
video
um if you're already subscribed thank
you so much and if you're not
go on ahead and hit that subscribe
button so today i'm-

[...]

i almost want to stop telling people that
i'm even ___ here or whatever the
case may be and i don't i don't even
really hold on to a letter
because i have a lot of different types
of ___ in my head
so i'm not going to sit up here and keep

holding on to type ___
it's like this and i'm not gonna sit up
and let people tell me like oh
i don't care i don't care what it looks
like to you that's what i am
that's what i am i'm someone that loves
my ___ that's what i am i don't care
what-

[...]

yo i promise you i don't care about that
i really don't
i just want healthy ___
that's it and me following people
with similar ___ is not going
to give me healthy ___ that's not what
it's going to give me
my ___ that's what i want i want a
fresh·clean ___ let me see these
___ that you're using using a ___
but you got ___ ___
oh let me watch that let me go ahead and
watch that because
your ___ type don't have absolutely
nothing to do with your ___

[...]

hello friends and/or family will do -
and welcome back to my youtube channel I
know I've been gone and I haven't been
posting in a long time and I get to hear
and make a bunch of excuses but that's
besides the point but today will be you
know me showing you guys my ___

routine so here is my ___ brush of the
shower you know after I ___
it did all that good stuff so without -

[...]

-so this is another
youtuber i don't follow her or whatever
not one of my faves you know and after i
heard
you know the video and her comments
about what she thought
about people that don't have ___ here
and we go back on that i'm sorry y'all
we'll be kind of like this is the
majority of what the video is about ___
typing my god
but she made some comments about
basically like ___ and ___ ___
should not be a part of the natural ___
community at all like
the ___ what else basically so i'm
going to play the clip um because
obviously my
unpopular opinion is that we should
right and i'm gonna explain to y'all
why i feel like we should be a part of
it
after we listen to the little clip so i
feel like you should watch the full
video-

[...]

i'm trying to figure out how that feels
on your ___ is it tingling

is it tingling how does it make you feel
do you feel good when you use this
___ is your ___ itching
okay your ___'s itching okay then you
know what i'm saying like
the focus we have to refocus because
what we focus on
ain't right but i ain't gonna say that
because at the end of the day you do
what you do
you do what makes you happy

[...]

STEP 1

i am very thick, so

i'm so stiff
I've been out i
normally never wear myself out and it's
so dry it's so gross and we're just
gonna have to
literally revamp my entire self i don't
know if y'all can hear that but

oh i'm so dry
i'm so dry y'all look at the back i'm
gonna show y'all
how i fix this y'all not ages oh no
but i'm just going to show you all the
products that i'm going to use for
the first thing i'm going to do this i'm
going to use this as like a pre-pro
to detangle myself this is amazing
stuff y'all

-to be washing this self we are doing a
pre-poo treatment we are -
we are giving ourselves tips and
tricks throughout the whole video so
make sure you stay tuned so let's get it
follow my instagram you know i'm all

about pre-pooing
-i'm starting to like pre-poo

oils because they really go in there and
dissolve the residues that
tangled and like makes me
hard to take apart

-number one pre-poof every time i wash my
self the night before i pre-poo myself
because
it just makes it a lot easier for me to
like detangle
and it just gives me that nice
moisturized protective layering before i
- i use these aloe leaves to pre-poo myself

pre-pulling is just a
treatment that you do before you -
yourself which gives you an extra
protective layer so today i'm going to
be using aloe i'm just cutting off the
pieces that i want and then i'm going to
trim off my ends as well and make sure
you rinse this plant before you start as well

-now I'm going in with the hot oil
treatment also from ___ and this is the
damaged one so this is the same one that
I've been using I've used it for three
uses now -

this hot oil
treatment is whoo life-changing honest
changing so this combo is what really
really gets me you guys can see how
good it looks and then I just go ahead

and I pulled that into myself and I let
that sit for about 10 minutes you guys

-after you have scooped out all the gel
of the aloe make sure you keep the
remainder of the aloe peace because
you're going to use that in the video as
you stay tuned you'll see what i'm
talking about so all you're going to do
is after you place everything in the
blender you're just going to blend it
until it's smooth

pre-poo yourself
i would not recommend going straight to
___ right after you've taken it down from a -

you will need 40
grams of fenugreek seeds
i love fenugreek seeds because it's high
in nicotinic acid
and nicotinic acid on myself dilates
the blood vesicles
it increases blood circulation and
increases the metabolic processes in the
self follicles
which in turn would prevent self loss
and-

all i'm doing now is just adding the gel
from the aloe into an applicator bottle
which makes it easier to distribute onto
myself then i'm going to add a couple
of my favorite oils the jamaican castor

oil i use the extra dark one which has
really helped thicken and strengthen
myself i'm going to use sweet almond oil
and i'm also going to be using avocado
oil and to help with the consistency of
the mixture i'm just going to add some
water as well and you also want to make sure you shake
this mixture very well

now that we have our pre-poo mixture
ready we can start applying it onto ourselves
so now i'm just taking this out and
you see I'm looking a little dry -

because you are brittle
and weak and you really want to make
sure that you at least
soften your cuticle with water and do a
light pre-poo
now me on the other hand i like to do a
light pre-poo which involves some type
of protein-

any sense bruh and for those of you who
don't know what pre-pooping is it's kind
of like we're setting up top home
security in ourselves i'm talking face
and motion detection night vision and
even a alarm system bruh like pre-porn
really just provides that extra layer of
protection to ourselves this is helpful
because during ___ I
experience the most amount of water
which can easily lead to protein loss

which also leads to frizziness dryness
and breakage
-pre-point helps by putting

a shield around yourself to prevent
them things from occurring and it also
protects yourself from ___ and to
put it blunt ___ are just maids
that have a stealing habit okay like
they come in clean up make sure
everything looks good but then strips
yourself from all of its moisture
that's just how it goes bro i don't make
the rules -

-so the items that i have with me when i
pre-poo are my aloe vera leaf
a knife to cut my aloe vera into chunks
a bowl to put the chunks into
now i have all of these pieces
here's the texture very kinky okay
so start off by taking just a piece
tie the rest of this mess up and now
that we're looking cute

take one of the pieces slice right
through the middle and you literally
want to dig your fingers
inside of yourself to get all of the juice out
so
i'm like pushing my fingers into myself and
all the juice is just coming out
and now i'm just rubbing the juice onto
myself really slippery

it just needs some reviving it needs
some moisture brought back to myself and

remember those pieces i told you to hold
off on those owl pieces we're about to
use those directly onto ourselves
by rubbing the aloe on myself it is
also helping to remove all the dirt and
buildup that was on myself aiding in
the - process
as well as giving moisture to myself
and a trick to get more gel out of the
aloe if you feel like it's gone just
poke little holes in yourself with your nails
and more gel will be exposed

once you are done blending your aloe all
you're gonna do is take a wave cap
stocking cap whatever you call a cap and
strain your aloe that way you don't have
chunks of aloe inside of yourself
so you're just gonna pour the gel inside
of yourself and gently squeeze it out
so now i'm just going to show you the
chunks of aloe that would have been in
yourself if you didn't strain that yeah
we don't want that
at all

-the more of this juice the better
because it's just easier for
the - or the - or whatever you're
using to slide through yourself
pulling out less of ourselves we don't want to
be pulling out ourselves because that's how
we don't grow and what's the
whole point of any of this if we aren't growing
push my fingers in
some more to get more juice out make
sure i'm getting the ends

I put a plastic bag over my head and I'm
gonna sit with this pre-poo for about 15
to 20 minutes so after I've applied the
bag I don't know
I like to get all the air out of the bag
I don't know if that makes a difference
but once I do that I put on a 100%
cotton t-shirt and you know just let myself
sit for about 15 to 20 minutes and let
that coconut oil penetrate me

I am very thick so
I do have to really rinse myself for a
minute for all of that coconut oil to
get out of myself then I take my-

I'm coiling up I'm getting some shrinkage
and that means I am hydrated
I'm soaking up the moisture I'm soaking up
the product and I am shrinking

once you've rubbed it on yourself just
massage yourself just massage yourself a little you
know get that aloe nice and worked into
that self you know
i trust me
you will thank me later okay
after i do that i just dump myself in
some warm water
and then i separate myself of course
sections are my best friend and now we

are going to prepare ourselves to add
the treatment onto ourselves

so i'm not very shrunken up cuz i'm still very
wet but I go ahead and I wash myself out
as you can see and make sure you wash yourself
out completely because you don't want
residue and then I use a towel and you -

I feel so nice after this process
you need to combine the two I'm telling
you I don't know how they work on their
own I just know that the combo works so
well on me so 10 minutes later I go
ahead and I take out myself and I'm
ready to ___ myself out you can see I am
still so hydrated

STEP 2

she's screaming but she's already coming back to life

detangle
her so i'll split her into workable
sections
and i use my tangle teezer as you guys
know i love my
tangle teezer and i'll just detangle her
i'm definitely now that she is a bit
longer
after i detangle each section i do twist
her up

to detangle her i find that when you
leave the ___ to sit in her
for a while it definitely
makes her much easier to detangle
and it definitely makes her feel a
lot more moisturized so
i just go in and i detangle from her tip
to her root

just go ahead and run my fingers through
her because that was not happening
before okay okay so that's just what i'm
doing throughout all of her look
this is no easy task okay

i i am going to
tie a few sections out
of the way and help lay
her down this is what
she looks like
without definition i
just kind of quickly
rubbed that through her and then i also
detangle with it as well
because it does provide
a lot of great slip so i
just kind of sprayed her
with water for her to
regain her shape and-

twist her up
detangle her from her
ends to her root making
sure everything is
completely detangled and
then i will twist her -

comes to detangling i
mainly start with my
hands so your fingers
are the cheapest tools
that you will ever have
and they were hearing her
that she is too naughty and-

-who's counting
I proceed to detangle her
and when it comes to detangling I
mainly start with my hands

- I don't know it's just something about it
like first of all when I apply it to her
she is too sticky like I think she is
super sticky and when I go to detangle
her it's harder for me to detangle
her for some reason like my ___
just sticks to one area and I have to
put so much force on her so I don't like
that at all

so your
fingers are the cheapest tools that you
will ever have and they're very
effective detangling her

so when I
use my fingers I can tell where her
tangles are

i began to separate her and twirled
her around my finger for maximum
definition"

she is extra gentle and I'm not ripping her out so I
always start with my fingers first and
once she is mainly detangled then I
go over her with a ___ just to make sure
that she is well detangle and then I
put her back into her twist
I would

always recommend
using a wide ___ I don't
recommend using anything smelter than
that to detangle her especially
because she is very delicate"

-a little bit more water
to that section and
begin to lightly finger
detangle not too much
just because i am going
to finger detangle more
once i am deep -
a little bit more water
to that section and
begin to lightly finger
detangle not too much
just because i am going
to finger detangle more
once i am deep
conditioning her
because she is stretched -

take down one big old section and finger detangle
can you guys see me finger detangling her with -
the - in it that's how you know okay and i
just wanted to reiterate that i do use the pads -
- on my fingertips and i just massage it into her
you don't want to use your fingernails or
you're just going to be scratching her up
as you guys can see she is looking shiny
she is popping that is what we want so next i'm -

I don't like how she feels when I
rinse her out she feels really dry
but then she gets really soft after you
let her sit for like a minute or two so
yeah I'm not really feeling this

you can see here I'm kind of like doing
the shingles is that it or finger
coiling I'm pretty sure you just finger
coiling I'm sorry my bad so I'm just
going in and I'm just finger coiling
her I don't think her coil every part of her
because if I did my my routine would be
tremendously longer than she is now but
yeah so just enjoy me finger coiling the
rest of her for this and this is
also in real time but this is in like-

-and
start the detangling
process and once i do
that i put on a 100 big
chopped or i just am
which i really love this
combination had called
best to get while she first up put her in - s
one more
water and i just put it
on her okay so when
i realized i like how
everything feels like
nice are just making a
little bit so long story
short i have started to
moisturize her on a
daily and she just
drastically changed i-

"detangle
so now i've got a smaller chunk in hand
so the best way to detangle is to start

from
her tips her ends and then work all the
way up to her root so that's what i'll
be doing

so there you go you can see
just holding her apart so i'm just
showing you her ends there
so some little bits are easier to do
than others so i'm just starting on a
little
section here off her main section

so what i'm doing is just teasing her and
pulling her apart with my hands
and just like that -

and now i'm just gonna part her down
her middle
to give myself two sections to work with

oops i ran into a tangle
okay got through that so yeah just
parting her down her middle
um i'm going to clip
up this side
and now for this half i'm going to
separate her
into two parts as well just to make it
easier for me to detangle because
i do not like detangling like that's the
worst part of ___

so yeah and now i'm just adding more

___

so now i'm just starting to detangle i'm
using a wide ___ and i'm just working my way up to the
roots
ah so i'm finally done this one baby-

see there she looks much much
better fully detangled
now we've got to tackle her left side
which looks
a little bit more uh
matted than her right side
most probably because this is the side
she lays on more
and she sleeps on her side so she does
get really
knotty so i'm just starting from the
bottom
and this time i'm working with the
___ completely because
it is just too difficult to try and get
her with my hands-

after raking the
products through her
with my fingers can
easily always start with
the most important part
as you can see she
is looking luscious
volume thick okay like i
am loving her right
now -

she's screaming okay she is but she's
already coming back to life oh we love
come on yeah this looks nice she looks
sexy we like her oh she juicy yes ma'am
she look fantastic

STEP 3

i'm gonna ___ my cousin about this

you guys i'm back after -
and let's just ___ we got a good one
off the first
couple of ___s because your girl is
tired
i'm tired i'm

as well so the -
___ my - still
moisturized and shiny
and soft which i really
___ and then i do ___
the diffuser and after i
___ some moisture over
and then just ___ that
to really ___ the
because my - is
already so oily i ___
it's one of the
downfalls about this so
about ___ and
conditioner can be sure
to ___ it a big thumbs
up and ___ down
below

this is the - that i'm going to be
___ in with i haven't ___ it yet but
my cousin she ___s the deep conditioner
for it and i ___ i ___ it one time
my - ___ it so i think i'm going to
try to ___ the -
and because this got avocado
and this has avocado in my - like
avocado these are my favorite this one's
old y'all
mine's still not ___ yet because i've
been ___ing mostly of this one but this
is my favorite

the Avalon organics and I ___ this
- so much it's no GMO it's vegan
and it's rosemary which ___ amazing I
___ the way it ___ my - smell and
___ and it has a bunch of healthy
benefit so now I'm just gonna wash wash
wash until I ___ like my - is
squeaky clean

so before ___ing i did ___ out the
pre-treatment and then i'm just going to
take a ample amount and i ___ to ___
on the outside of my - and then ___
my way on the inside so i just ___ to
___ my roots ___ it on ___ that
- nice and acquainted with my
scalp you ___ me

um i am ___ in with the first -
we all ___ the first - doesn't ___
what it ___ to ___

it's just you gotta ___ the first one
out of the way to really ___ to where
you ___ to be you ___

while I was ___ing this I
actually purposefully ___ a ton of
- and this is because I ___ my
- was still moisturized it still was
___ing good and I'm like okay what's
the catch
when is my - gonna ___ out so I
actually ___ a ton of - just
to ___ if my - was going to ___ out

and also when i - my -
i ___ to ___ this little scalp ___r
thing ___ blood flow up there and
it's actually really good for -
growth as well
so i ___ to ___ that and it really like
___ rid of the dead skin cells up there
and all that kind of stuff

then i ___ to go
inside my scalp ___ing section by
section to ___ sure that i ___ my scalp
as clean as i can on the first
try and i also ___ in a downward motion
that way i'm not ___ng up my roots
which will ___ it harder to ___

this is the first one i'm ___ing
it's been really dry and I'm going to
___ that section of my - and then
after your two hours and my - has
___ so this is what it ___ like
when it was wet it ___ me the basics

___ing and ___ing my - so I ___
the -
which I ___ it has been an OG I really
___ it because not only does it our
thoroughly ___ my - with one to
two washes it also ___ my -
___ing moisturized not stripped of its
moisture

and you'll ___ that I still
have and I'm able to ___ my kinky
coily coil ease throughout the whole
process which is a sign of healthy -
so I definitely ___ that this -
has ___ a part in ___ my 4c
- and I___ some of you guys are
gonna ___ in the comments section and
___ with me ___ing this is not 4c -
but you ___ what I will ___ you in the
comment section okay alright ___ing on
to the next step

and then i ___ the gel that
___s sure i ___ ahead and ___ this
and it's able to you basically form the
curls and stuff like that so that's
why i ___ to ___ this once a week and
then we're gonna ___ from there

so before ___ing i did ___ out the
pre-treatment and then i'm just ___ to
___ a ample amount and i ___ to ___
on the outside of my - and then ___
my way on the inside so i just ___ to
___ my roots ___ it on ___ that
- nice and ___ with my
scalp you ___ me

when i’m ___ing my - i ___ to
___ on the scalp
___ing the - in and making sure
to ___ rid of any product buildup that
may be there
after i ___ my scalp i ___ to ___
on the length of my - ___ing sure to
drag the - down the strands
while lightly ___ing with my fingers
i ___ this twice and then ___ on to
conditioner

because it is very very important
because i just ___ to ___ me still
___ my - this is what it ___
___ when it’s done my -
___ like
i didn’t ___ that again I just don’t
even ___ my - with warm water in it
and ___ it ___ soft and smooth it
doesn’t ___ your - -

and then i ___ the gel that
___s sure i ___ ahead and ___ this
and it’s able to you basically form the
curls and stuff like that so that’s
why i ___ to ___ this once a week and
then we’re gonna ___ from there

can ___ my - so it
s a little bit more
voluminous with ___
your - you ___ to
___ sure that you do

___ it into your
scalp or at least ___
up whatever debris is on
your scalp to ___ it
for ___ing

for so my - is already so i'm going to
___ up my cuticle and tips you can
use the ___ off and then I ___ the
remaining - so i don't ___ if it's
like a cream with glitter and then I
___ myself a nice scalp ___
as well

but as soon as i ___ it to my - i
was ___
it ___ up so quickly like
within two seconds it was already a
thick foamy lather which i
absolutely ___ and for some reason
it had some slip to it so here you're
gonna ___ me i sort of ___ my fingers
through my - which i would
never ___ with any other - so that
was
quite impressive for me so yeah i'm just
gonna ___ with
all four of my sections and ___ in
the -
um usually i don't - ___ through
my ends but my - was really really
dirty -

so after i'm done ___ing the
product out it's time to ___ in with my
favorite - the gold series from

pantene moisture boost i ___ it all
around my scalp as you can see here i
___ sure i really ___ in there because
my - was dirty i'm not even gonna ___
to you y'all saw how much product was in
it in the beginning of this video so ___
the kitchen area ___ all over there
maybe ___ in a little too hard on the
- but after i'm done ___ my
scalp i do ___ sure i bring the -

___ing on to the
- so this one is
like a jail i have a lot
of crap in there and it
s always ___ ___ a
little stretched of -
but i just ___ some comb
through my - to
___ it and
___ the product

two clean - and i'm just ___ing
you guys the texture
first of all i was ___ that it
___ in a tub
and then i was also ___ by the
consistency
it almost ___ slimy like but i ___ it
is because
um it ___ have aloe vera in the
ingredients list so
i ___ that adds to the consistency

so
i just ___ it through my whole entire
- shaft
so i would ___ if your - isn't
that dirty
then just ___ the - on your roots
but if you ___ the need to then of
course you can ___ whatever suits you

after you ___ it out
and i was ___ with this
scrub-a-dub dub
and ___ing out all of that - the

I wasn't ___ a whole lot from this
- and conditioner I ___ it was
just kind of you ___ gonna be like any
other - and conditioner but I was
wrong and I'm very happy to ___ I was
wrong because this is no ordinary
- this right here this is the holy
grail of - I ___ as soon as it
___ my head that this was going to
be the - I ___ to ___ for the
rest of my life

- did not this - hydrated my -
it ___ it it had those suds that I
absolutely ___ honestly I couldn't ___
for anything more from a - than
this has to ___ so after my magical
- experience I ___ to ___ out

so here is that second - and i
___ i ___ my - a third time i
typically ___ two to three -
so yes this is the third - you ___
those white sides that's how you ___
your - is going to be nice and clean

oh it ___ good too oh it ___ good
oh my goodness
y'all in this - baby
i'm about to ___back and ___ the whole
line if they ___ like this
my - ___ good my - ___
really good oh my goodness i'm gonna
___ my cousin about this

STEP 4

never ever ever ever ever forget yourself okay

let's be honest you're looking uh you're
looking a little messy you're looking a
little bit
dry sahara desert vibes and

as y'all can see you were just
looking a little bit for eggs but the
rest of you is definitely 4b4c
as y'all already know wash day is a day like
literally a day so if you don't got your tunes
and you ain't dancing you're gonna be bored
your feet gonna be hurting you can be thinking
about the pain of this day but yeah you just had
to dance it out

so y'all actually love this ___
was like your second time using it and
there's so much slip and it also smells
amazing so yeah you're just gonna take down
your section and go in with ___
trust your that's not all you use you just
kept going in and going in and going in
because like ___ deep
___ is like the best dip of
like your entire wash day like this is
where you come alive guys like
this is where everything happens

deep ___ can penetrate your
shaft a lot more effectively this is
also an important step to take because
build-up can cause dryness breakage and
dull you

the second step is to deep
___ with heat so fully saturate
you with any deep ___ of
your choice

so finally after hours and hours and
hours you're deep ___ so you're
just putting it up so that you can finally
put on your eating cap which is actually a
plastic bag loll and you do this to keep
you in motion and keep in heat while what
deep ___ so that the product
works

you know it's been like day 28 without
washing you so you're
super dry and you really need to deep
___
get some moisture back into you and
allow you to be moisturized because when
you're dry
you're more successful susceptible to
damage

it's all basically predominantly to
moisturize so kind of similar to Drive
remedy a lot of their products you love
but they've got silicones in and you're not
you don't hate silicones but if you're not
washing you regularly it can be

hard to remove them from you so you'd
rather just not use them so yeah that's
what you like about this ___s
there's no silicones in it and it's
really good at moisturizing it's really

___ right after using
this ___ by
saturating you to
you so you want to
see it did this video
look at this like all you
have on you ends you have
low porosity sometimes
your type you know your needs to be healthy

Pizza and hydrate baby hydrates
and then you dry you with the t-shirt
instead of a towel because you will snag
you and they braid you and
trust your like you may not see it but in
the long run like they just adjust
things because of the house just then go
in with ___

now going in with your absolute favorite
deep ___ at the moment you're gonna
go ahead and use it to detangle and
hydrate you but you guys if you could
say like this deep ___ smells so
amazing you wish you could describe to you
like how good it smells it's really
great for making you pop it makes
you nice and hydrated and it smells so
good that you feel like it turns youinto like an aromatherapy

session going in with your brand spanking
new tangle teezer

so natural club sent your three of their
ice cream ___ deep ___s to
use
the first one that you're showing you all
is the repairing wheat in argan oil ice
cream ___
this one is going to replenish you

yours is a DIY deep
___ made out of avocado and
banana but if this was any other day say
like your lazy wash day if you haven't
seen that video you'll go ahead and link
that in the description box below you

the second one is the curl defining
flaxseed and acai
ice cream ___ this one is to
prevent frizz retain moisture
and to elongate you the one that
you're going to be using is original dry
solution
lavender and tea tree ice cream this is
a deep ___ that's going to

the side of you
already sectioned this
off and then you deep
___ with a
smaller section you deep
___ in quadrants i
start off with a sizable
amount of ___ on

the length of you
that it was looking real
rough and

for a long time so one of your favorites
the ___ is a different story you
have loads that you absolutely love and you
will alternate between ___s or just
like a regular ___ the sort
common thing between all your ___s
is they're all quite thick they're all
quite rich so you don't really use
anything that's like

it this ___ is good if
you are protein
sensitive and low
porosity like your because
this ___ has no protein
in it you

the ___ you
use the most at the moment is the evader
Newt replenish ___ this is the
deep moisture version so they have to
they have a light one and a deep one and
you use the deep one the most and they did
send this to your a little while ago they
launched it you think that's beginning of
this year but they sent it to your last
year and yeah you just really love using
you just feel so much softer

you're gonna go ahead and distribute the
deep ___ throughout you
you could totally tell its new because

obviously you're not even holding the
handle you're gonna use it to distribute
the deep ___ really well and

own instead of your having
to spray it with a spray
bottle dried you with a
damp towel and then i
applied the product
generously you use it then
and really allow that
deep ___ to
penetrate your ears and
still make sure to
detangle and

and it s the shea
moisture curl and shine
___ and you use this
in the ___ as well
and then when you go ahead
and you wash it and right
after you wash you do this
method and you like to use
a deep ___ but
it was time you just to
use a wide tooth comb

and then you want you guys to
never ever ever ever ever forget yourself okay
put that ___ on yourself don't forget it and
you also need to get the back and put it on that
kitchen and make sure you are moisturized just as
much as the rest of you so you take a baggie

to do now
yourself in here to
kind of lock in the
moisture that should
already be in you when
you have already like i
think um you think you
speak for yourself you kind
of want to become a
stretch natural but i
just know as soon as i
leave the house you like
with the aussie moisture
minute deep ___

my diy steamer to
deep ___ rather
than just letting you sit
with heat
this is how you
look when all of that
product is rinsed out so

you never use those ___ caps or whatever you never
even have those you just take a bag an old bag that
i've used previously and put it on you and
take your ___ all right y'all so after you have
taken your ___ and fully cleaned myself you am
going to be taking out yourself and literally
just using the water to wash out that ___
and you do make sure that you get all
of the product out of you by
just literally saturating it in water

so
that's when you're now detangling finally

detangling and this is the base B of Y
tooth comb but it's been a year and you
can't find it so you're just using an afro
comb you're doing for anyone you told you to
do so that's law

then take your
white tooth comb and
always start from your
ends to your root making
sure everything is
completely detangled and
then you will twist that
section and you start with

First day but this is
how you look right
after deep ___
you literally just
finished two using a
detangler it's okay
did this amazing wow

did
you like what you
look like after a few
days of ponytails and
braids and styling with
you and you love my
favorite you has dried

well just to open up your
cuticles and allow the
deep ___ to

penetrate deeper within
you but to
put it simple bruh it
basically just helps the
___ get in you
and get all through you

so now you just took it
out of your bonnets and you
looks like ramen love
that you smell so good
you look like you
know you like a jelly
the jelly type of
products work better for
you as you can see i
am done with the
___ that you put in
you on your face i

but y'all look at you like oh your gosh this
___ you're telling you don't ever saying put
you on but next you're just going to move on to

you had a j cole
in the video make sure
you get it on the end of
yourself all you have to
focus on you a lot
because you definitely try
and to find any products
works for for your type

STEP 5

okay we lied, here's the actual last step

yo we remember
being like a five six year old and our
mom would sit here and grease or is that
is that the terminology like grease
Moscow yeah yeah grease our schedule and
use this to stop our ___ when we used to
have our little ___ and our little
___ and all that good stuff

ones in the back back here because our
___ texture in the back is a little bit
more loose than the rest of our ___
and one last time we're gonna go ahead
and use the Denman ___ and just clomp
our ___ together just to make sure that
we really coated all our ___ and if the
product is evenly distributed the last
product we're using is blueberry blitz by

is this blueberry ___ blueberry bliss ___ and
shout cream we're glad we didn't try to say that fast
now this product smells fire okay yes okay so
we're going to take some of this put it on our hand
so we're going to take our denman ___ and we're
going to ___ it on our ___ just to give
ourselves one smooth and really good detangle

now if we're blessed with the same crow
pattern all throughout our ___ then
we can totally skip the step but sadly
the ___ in our front and our face do not
___ the same as everywhere else and
it's not heat damage we barely put will
ever basically put heat on our ___

so this
product is a og and it is trending so I
said let me just try far it has
pretty successful our ___ feels very
nice and moisturized and we don't think
that these ___ are necessarily gonna
unravel we always have issues with the

so that our ___ style can come out right
the more detangled our ___ is while we're doing
this the easier the takedown process would be
the more smooth our ___ will look the better

it would look like the less frizz we'll have
all together we would just come together really
really good so now that we have that all
throughout
our ___ ___ we are going to start the ___

when we style and ___ up our ___ we use
the lco method which stands for ___
we use a total of five
things when we style our ___

styling method a ___ we believe this is
called a rat toothed ___ we don't know
if that's the proper name for it but
something like this and something like
this we don't know the name of this kind
of ___ but we call it like a padded
___ whatever so we're gonna be using
this for smoothing and this for parting
this is important because of the fact
that these ___

the Shea Moisture styling jelly and this
is actually a product that we decided to
pick up when we was at the ___ store no
specific reasoning to be honest we was
just like oh a jelly we know we want a
product that's probably gonna hold but
not gonna keep our ___ stiff so we went
for this jelly and since it has been a

trend on weTube to start using a
wonderful og product
so the first
thing that we use is our diy spray
camille rose lavender ___
___ main crush unicorn ___
cream beautiful textures ___ definer styling
custard lastly agave spray treatment argan oil
so those five things in that order is all
that we use

so what we will need to do is just make sure
that
our roots this is the key to this ___
out we want to make sure that the roots
are taut we're ___ pretty tall at the root
and then when we continue going down we
want to
make sure that our ___ stays detangled
okay

___ now we use about this much as we're
sharing ___ to one side of our ___ and
it smells so so good literally smells
like blueberry Jolly Ranchers and I
really love the smell of this product so
what the judges of course it defines
our ___ and make them pop really
helps also with the frizz and

it took us
a really long time to find me a gel that

doesn't get our ___ crunchy but it
really keeps our ___ together if we
get what we're saying so this product is
definitely if that's what we're looking
for and as we see here we're also using
that raking motion to distribute the
___ product

so we're gonna go ahead and
scrunch our ___ trying to not scrunch
really hard where we're causing frizz but
just to help encourage our ___ to pop
more

now that we are detangles damp and
moisturize we can start shingling so
ideally the shingle method is we're
sectioning our ___ into a small
section taking our ___ ___ by
___ and applying the product through

so what we're going to do is take a
___ cream or gel apply it to the
small section and we want to rake it
through the ___ first so we want to
rake it through the ___ like we
normally do with product now we're
going to start taking small pieces to
where they almost appear as a single
___ of ___

also another thing that we
learned is when applying like styling
products and stuff like that making sure
that we just keep the styling products on
the ends of our ___ and not the scalp
and just leaving products like this that
strictly say that are for the scalp when
the scalp that's helped me a lot to we
because we remember we used to put a lot

it's just our ___ can be really thick
especially towards the back of our ___
so we're taking about that much for
these ___ we're gonna add up some
show focus that on the end Swiss do not
unravel if we apply enough gel to the
ends that's why we stress this for a
___ especially if we want to keep
them in for a considerable amount of
time we want to make sure that they
hold well with enough product so once my
product is in we're going to start doing
our two ___ ___ which is very simple
it looks harder than it is

we're just gonna rub the
piece so like rub the product over the
___ and it's really soaking into the
___ so whatever our ___ pattern is
it's gonna bring it to the forefront so
what we're doing gets coercing our
natural ___ pride into really pop

so now that we got the ___ ing cream and
the gel we're gonna get another gel um
these are they're different because this
one is like a jelly and it makes our
___ soft so it's not gonna harden our
___ which we really like about it but is
gonna make sure our ___ is in place
this is one of our favorite so it doesn't
make our ___ really crunchy and like
all stiff it keeps our ___
of product so yeah with the ___
we make sure we're focusing on our ends
because that's the oldest part of our
___ it's the deadest part of our ___
and it needs the most moisture and
care to allow our ___ to grow after we
add a whole bunch of ___ into our

___

we put us into a little bun and entrap
ourselves
into a nice plastic cap and then we'll
sit under a dryer this is not necessary
for everybody but for me we have low
porosity ___
so our ___ needs that heat to open up
the ___ shafts and so the moisture can
get inside our ___

steam our ___ which we don't see a lot of
people on weTube doing but because my
___ is so thick and coarse and dry

we need to steam our ___ versus just
putting on like a heated cap because
steaming actually lifts the follicles or
the cuticles on each ___ of our ___
and allows that ___ to get into
our ___ and really moisturize our
___ and lock in that moisture
so that's
why we really love steaming versus just
putting on we know a towel or a cotton
t-shirt and walking around the house I
like to steam it and really allow that
moisture to penetrate into each of our
___ ___ to keep that moisture
throughout the week so this is what our

___ looks like after steaming and we
feel so pillow soft we get oh gosh we
feel so soft we just we can't we can't
stop touching our ___ after that we rinse
our ___ and we use warm water to rinse
our

going in with the Shea Moisture jamaican
black castor oil ___ ___
and just going to apply that in our
entire ___ and just finger ___
ministers and we use this generous
amount

yeah we just basically added until our
___ feels really saturated with it now
we're just taking this kinky ___ y ___ ing
custard and its new and just removing
the cover from it yeah there was someone
to cover so we're just going to use that
as well

___ are looking like
as we can see around the front and the
sides in the back of our ___ that were
pulled up in the ___ it was looking
a little stretched
so what we're going to do is we're just
going to take some water in a spray
bottle
and we're just going to spray around the
front and back of our ___
just to allow it to we know shrink up
and activate those ___

don't waste our product now we're just an
hour of that all overnight here and we're
not using a lot because a little goes a
long way and we just want to make sure
it's all evenly distributed in our ___
and we just use our DIY a mix and we're just
going to fluff my
out a little bit

as we can see as usual
anaglyphic up out of our ___ so we had to
go in with a little bit more product so
yeah so we're just kind of like fluffing
it out because sometimes when we do
___ we gets a little straight still

look at how much our ___ just shrinks up
and it's still wet so
if we were to let this dry we would
shrink up like all the way up here

while we're ___ ing it down we like to put
our finger there so it like it clumps the
___
a lot better and then we grab them again
and see how they're like really clumped
together what we do is we shake it
oh there's a lot of product on there
but anyways we just like to shake them

so this is day one we really like how
voluminous our ___ is because day one my
___ is usually smaller
so yeah we're excited to see what our ___
looks like
tomorrow because we're definitely gonna
pop up a lot more

oh
and we also reached our little patch a lot

of people ask me about our patch and why
we decided to go ___ in this one
section and the truth of the matter is
there is no specific reason we just
wanted to have something a little bit
different something that stands out and
so we bleached a little patch of our ___
that's it so basically what we're going to
be doing is parting our ___ we don't know

now for the styling part um it's super
easy because we're literally just going to
put it back into the two ___ that i
had in the beginning of the video
um at this point we don't even do like a
clean part or anything we just use the
part that we have
um and yeah we're just gonna
put some ___ ___ in put
some grease and then
put some oil

so we just go in ___ it out this is what
we're looking like
we're looking very nice yes ma'am so we're
just gonna take our big scrunchie
and we are going to flip our ___ upside
down and put it in a pineapple because i
we're doing this
overnight and we're just going to show we
guys how we do it

so we put our ___ up in a pineapple or
just a really really high ___ right
on the top of our head
we take a head scarf and we fold it
diagonally so that it forms the shape of
a triangle
just like this
and we put it over the back of our head
like so
and then we just pick our head up and i
cross it over our head just like this
and then we just tie it at the back

and this is really good because it
prevents any tug or pull when we sleep
and it just keeps our ___ really nice
and intact
so this is what we're looking like and
we're gonna come back the next day to show
we guys the takedown

all right we guys so it is now the
following day and we're just taking off my
head scarf and just preparing to take my
___ down and just show we guys what i
do

so once we take out our ___ we just give
ourselves a good shake
we know we flip around a couple times
get it nice and loose
and this is what we're looking like

straight out of the scrunchies straight
out of the head scarf this is what we

um our ___ also was not 100 dry so we
just went in with our diffuser
anyways we're just gonna go right ahead
and diffuse
normally we don't diffuse we let it air
dry but since we did do this overnight
and it was

we know still a little damp and just
we know for the sake of time we decided
that we was going to just
diffuse the ___ we did that for about 15
minutes and this is what it was looking
like

all right last and final step is to
fluff and shape ___
we feel like it's a pretty visual thing
just make sure we're fluffing
our roots only and not through the ends
of our ___
[Music]

okay we lied here's the actual last step
so sometimes if we want our ___ to lay a
certain way

we'll use pins just to uh kind of just
pin our ___ down so we stay that way

that's what we're doing for our banks here
just to create that look
and yes this is what our ___ looks like
we're just gonna shape it a little bit
more but

um sometimes we just get our ___ ___
and then we put a wig back on but
obviously we're wearing our natural ___
out today so we was planning to wear our
natural ___
so we just ___ up our ___ so it would
stretch out
and then the next day we un___ it and
then we did a ___ out

we want to typically
keep in our ___ for a few days if not
longer so we want to make sure that
our parts look nice and neat rather
than just being like all over the place
which we've tried before and it did not
work out well so we definitely
recommend
using some sort of ___ to part and then
a ___ flatten our cuticle if our
___ is frizzy and unruly like mine can

EXHIBIT A: RESULTS

how could you ever sleep on your type four curls

these are my final results i am
literally in love with my hair like the
definition the fullness like it's thick
up in there too y'all and whenever my
hair gets to this point sometimes i just
wonder myself how did i ever have like i
wouldn't say i had a hate for my hair
but i i didn't love it at one point in
my life and now it's just like easy how
could you ever sleep on your type four
curls like do y'all see

=

and now because i need the results asap
i would usually air dry my hair but this
time i'm using my diffuser
on the warm setting
and now with my eco cell gel i'm gonna
go ahead and slick down
any sections that i feel like needs
looking down
get these flyaways you know
and now for my edges you know i gotta go
in with the
og certified bella palmad

and although i love definition i love
volume
as well so i'm gonna use my white comb
just to get a little bit more volume
in this wash and go
and this is the results beauties let me
know in the comments what did you think
about my wash and go routine like is it
too complicated
is it easy to follow would you try out
my washing a routine like if you do not
have one
if you enjoyed this video please leave a
thumbs up for me
it's really appreciated and it's free
and if you haven't as yet
subscribe to my channel because i post
content like this all the time

=

alright so this is what my final results
look like I'm an addict
I'm sad think I wanna put down because
this little piece though trying to play
me I don't know my sister but I do like
the jail don't like it over the other do
I feel like I feel like it's even which
is good for me you know I can be able to
jump back and forth between in jail I
just finished this little piggys flip it
acting raggedy okay but yeah but here
doesn't feel hard which is good that's a
positive my hair any crunchy why only I
want a question because I want to go
crunch a bunch on me but like I'm just

wondering okay not a problem at all
we're gonna lay down these edges though
I need a scarf to put away I think we go
to the south part for the people today

=

[Music]
alright guys so these are the final
results from all the products I'm going
to let my hair air dry for probably
about 30 minutes and then I'm gonna go
ahead and start defusing and then once
I'm all dried and ready to go I'll come
back and show you guys stuff on the
results and my final thoughts on these
products alright guys so these are the
final results of today's washing though
today's Washington was full of surprises
for me I actually wasn't expecting half
of these products to do as well as they
did this is probably one of the best
wash gos I've had well this is certainly
in the best watching though I've had all
of 20/20 so let's just go with that one
of the styling products that actually
surprised me the most was this Aussie
gel I was expecting this to be really
sticky and leave a residue since it is
such a thick gel but none of that
happened luckily it is not sticky at all
it is soft it is defined it is amazing
it definitely dried with a very hard
cast which is what I personally like but
once I diffused all of the cast out I'm
just left with a perfectly soft and

defined wash and go overall this whole
wash day routine from wash to styling to
finishing it came out absolutely amazing
I hope if you guys pick up any of these

=

and voila this is the end results guys
um I went for a basic braid out I didn't
want to do any fancy styles and hello
definition hello moisture hello shine
hello everything thank you so much for
watching love you guys until next time

=

here are the results everyone as you can
see
oh definition is absolutely popping
so is volume got my spirals back
you guys all enjoyed today's wash
routine and got some valuable
information out of it
please click the link um if you want to
try the functional beauty customizable
shampoo and conditioner which i
absolutely love and i mean the results
really speak for themselves thank you so
much for watching and i'll see you back

you know so i feel like edge entity gets
the trinity tick okay i definitely feel
like their products do what they say
they do so yeah i'm excited to see how
much more my hair grows throughout the
month i am gonna continue to use their

products obviously i've just run out of
their capsules but i will be using the
follicle stimulant on my hair until it
probably finishes so yeah we're gonna
see if there's any more drastic progress
i'm excited as you guys saw from the
results their products definitely have
an effect on promoting hair growth so
yeah i hope you guys enjoyed this video
i will be of course linking all the
products that i used down below in the
description box as well as my discount
code so you guys can get some money off
your own purchase just in case you want

=

okay so now I'm done picking out my hair
this is my hair please right
freshly defused and this is the results
of my products gave me so my hair is
super defined big bouncy it's not
crunchy even my dip Adele in it but it's
not crunchy and it's very soft um and
yeah this is it so thank you for
watching I leave any videos that you
guys would like to see down below in the
comment section don't forget to Like
comment and subscribe to see more of

=

so this is my final look obviously i am
loving my hair
um you know i beat my face a little bit
put on some hooked earrings and that's

it so i'm loving this extreme wet line
gel like my hair is 80 dry and it just feels
so soft it smells good my curls are popping
you cannot go wrong with this product so
i would definitely recommend it
and yeah anyways thank you so much for
watching
like always don't forget to subscribe to
my channel for more natural hair videos
and a lot of different content i am so
close to 30k

=

the results speak for themselves and
look at the cow pattern on the hair it
looks so bouncy so shiny and I think of
it to be using this method from now on
because a little does go a long way with
castor oil and sometimes gel isn't
always the best way to define your hair
so I really do think costo helps to
preserve your extensions next I just
went ahead and done my edges and tied it
with a silk scarf to keep it out of the
way and help lay them down
this is what the hair looks like when
it's fully defined it looks amazing now
once the hair has dried this is what it
looks like and if you're subscribed to
my channel you know that I love big and
fluffy hair so I just took a afro pick
and picked out some of those curls now
this is the end result guys I can't
believe you can get this much definition
from just oil anyway guys now it's my

time to love you and leave you I hope
you really enjoyed this video thank you
for watching I would love it if you

=

so these are my twist out results you
can see that my curls are super defined
really love twist outs for that reason
because it really helps to prevent your
natural curl from developing a lot of
frizz and my hair especially gets very
frizzy when it's naturally curly so I
love twists for that reason twists are
super good and preventing frizz and also
providing definition to your curls so if
you guys haven't tried this yet I
definitely recommend it it's so good I
don't know how this would work on looser
hair types like straight hair or wavy
hair I don't know but for curly hair for
naturally curly hair it works super well
do if you guys have not already please
remember to subscribe so that you do not
miss any future videos every Monday and

=

really do like this final look of my
hair you guys like and now as the days
go on throughout the week it will get
bigger and we get fluffier just because
I am a wild sleeper but my tip to you
guys um for like at nighttime what I
would do is just like wrap it up with a
scarf just so that the curls can kind of

stayed managed and like down to the head
and then in the morning like I said I
would just revamp it by wetting it which
helps to reactivate the products and

=

and here is the final result looking
beautiful
super curly we air dry her hair so we
try to use a minimal heat or no heat i
hope you enjoyed this video and give a
little like if you like it and subscribe

EXHIBIT B: GENERATED TRANSCRIPTS

curls are popping!

welcome to my channel it
s me to wash out of my
hair so i want to mainly
focus on my roots
because once i rinse the
shampoo off it s going
to be a college video
and you guys should
check that video out i
will see you guys in my
next video bye everyone

welcome back to my
channel it s me to wash
out of my hair so i had
to go in with a spray
bottle which has only
water in it and make
sure the hair is fully
saturated in the with
the conditioner and
after i rinse my hair
out a little bit before
i start to shampoo i
think the scalp is still
wet and it really helps

me to cleanse it and get
that off so yep that s
what i was doing and i
think i like it more
than i like all of my
favorite part which is
the water cuz i was just
like you know in my zone
in the bathroom just to
snip my hair watching
like i said i just braid
it back and let that sit
for a few minutes
alright so this is what
my hair looks like after
a few days of ponytails
and braids and styling
with it and i love my
hair how i do this as
you can see i am feeling
myself i do think
although my hair does
have like a shape to it
i feel like i said in
the beginning of the
time like all people do
is talk about shea
moisture and they talk
about um well they look
at that let me know down
below and if you want me
to try anything else
with this comb also let
me know if you guys have
any questions hair
related or not hair like

okay so now I'm just going to take my
scalp and i'm just going to give you
guys a brief explanation of basically
what they thought it would be easier to put on my
scalp
i don't think that this is what it was
a lot of them botd on freshly washed
I happens a lot of different types of
hair in the shower i washed it conditioned
her hair is moisturized so now I'm gonna
get my own kata brush your own hair
growth as well as the first time is
you just use a little bit of water to
have my friend and the roots of my
hair and the circumference of this hair
so if you guys want to see how I style my
hair after i do what I'm doing here
so now I'm just gonna take my Cantu
moisturizing curl activator cream and
I'll see you in my next one

hey guys welcome back to my channel it's
basically it for this hair type is what i've
tried on the scalp the time and then
I just go ahead and start defusing and
shine let me know down below in the
description box below I would say
it looks like a little bit more
so i'm gonna be doing a wash and
go there's a lot of information
in your hair so it was super dry and
so what I do is I got the shower
i did want to make sure that every
strand is that the conditioner is a little tight
something that i love the shampoo
in the next one

bye love you guys i've been using
this styling cream of hair but
it's looking at the end look at that and then as
many pieces and stuff like this
and i will see you guys in my next video

welcome to my channel my
name is lex legs and
tangles it s out of the
loose ponytail this is
going to be my fall and
very possibly winter
wash day routine whole
thing i can be applying
product to kind of give
it the effects and as if
you know it really is
wet and then you can go
ahead and take it out
and style it into your
desired style today i
wanted to do my hair
this is how it looks
join me next week for an
in - depth tutorial on
that and i will link it
but um it just gets
really on the ends to my
curls for the scalp kind
of just making sure that
the last piece that you
want to be in the video
yeah so like it just
looks so cute i have
noticed that my nails
have been growing a lot

faster obviously it
really is the the end of
this video so thank you
so much for watching and
i will see you guys in
my next video bye guys

hey guys welcome back to my channel
today i'm going to be using the
hair so if you want to put a lot
of product on my hair and I'm using the
shea moisture shampoo and conditioner
it's still going to be a little bit
of the back of my head and stay
tuned in the comment section below what you're here
i love this in the morning so if you want to do
my hair
in the back of my hair and then
I just use this to this point in
so yeah that's what I'm going to do is I
don't know if you guys have any
questions all the time i wash my hair
like this is a thick but yeah it's
not good my hair it's the takedowurated and then you can start off by taking
products so
that is my hair smooth and then I
just worked into the scalp and
we're going to be using for the
benefits of this part of my hair with a
lot of people that expensive and then I got my
natural curl curly hair products
and then I just want to show you guys the
best thing to do is I want to make sure that you
get into the shower i was a very
drop in the shower and then i'll
move on to the next process would be the

shampoo and conditioner and then I wash it out and
then i just take my scalp and I'm
just going to take out after that we're
still going to be using this one of the
conditioner is the bottom in the
morning so now I'm just gonna go
ahead and rinse the shampoo in
the back of my hair this is the
same thing on the shampoo that
i'm going to go ahead and section my hair
this is the best one
the hair like if you guys have
any questions let me know if you
guys can see my hair is short I
just like to do this and to figure out
and then I just use this to the
section the hair so if you look like
this color lays like i can describe to my
channel

oil if you have tried this product
will be amazing for the back to the
transfuer like i said this is the results
they don't feel heavy and i want to
keep the product in between the layers
that has to grow and it just makes my curls
this is a hair rake it moves after my
forehead to look smaller but just to
end up here trying to
convince myself that my edges are quite
fine the hair and then i'll be back
with the shampoo process it just keeps
my hair really soft and it was
a year six bouncing bouncing back

hey guys welcome to my
channel my name is lex
legs and they can break
through my hair so i can
also do this because it
makes my hair so
extremely soft so i add
a little bit more water
to that section and
begin to lightly finger
detangle not too much
just because i am going
to finger detangle more
once i am deep
conditioning my hair
because i usually use
the wrapping papers as
you can see as usual now
it stops frizz but i
will see you guys in my
next video bye hey guys

welcome back to my
channel it s me to wash
out of my hair so i want
to mainly focus on my
roots because once i
rinse the shampoo off it
s going to be a college
video and you guys
should check that video
out i will see you guys
in my next video bye hey

guys welcome to my
channel my name is lex

legs and they can break
through my hair so i can
also do this because it
makes my hair really
soft and it smells
amazing the next thing i
got was the on hand so i
wet my hair because it s
stretched so you can see
i like to do i like to
have my hair dripping
wet and i like to do
this so i can slowly
work my hair into a
downward motion because
i have to keep things
like it get it and then
you also have like you
have to dry it or
anything but i want to
make sure that you have
a shirt on that you guys
saw me apply the leave -
in conditioner i take
some of this oil just to
help me with the
takedown of my braids in
my hair for about 15
minutes and this is what
it s looking like on its
own so i really like of
that my hair is like dry
it s still they go
because it also helps
with me to put a look at
that shine like gel and

a little goes a long way
and it really glides
through the hair i was
so amazed and it s so
thick it with my hands
just to make it more
easy as you can see here
i am parting my hair
into four sections and
then we would just go
part in your hair will
make sure you get the
back of the head too
because you know we have
curls here we still got
hair here same thing i
just figure comb it and
then i scrunch it back
up so like in the
morning time if i find
my hair is like super
frizzy cuz your girl is
a wild a products a lot
to work in one way to it
so first that section we
are done and i will see
you in my next video bye

hey guys welcome to my
channel today i am deep
conditioning my hair
because it s stretched
so you can see i like to
do i like to have my
hair dripping wet and i
like to do is very key

to that you really want
to make sure that you
have even   like that
hold on my edges and and
i think this is because
of the mask so i would
definitely recommend it
and yeah anyways thank
you so much for watching
and i will see you guys
in my next video bye hey

hi everyone it's always started I'll
get blow dry my hair i do my own trims
so i'm just gonna put that throughout
your hair so it can fit and shingle
strand is absolutely ridiculous I actually
felt like the person that you can see how the
hair pick is any more of a treatment
and it just makes it a lot easier for
the water on and really just dresses
well her below so you can kind of see
them as you guys seemed hair but you
know what i'm saying the whole thing
every step

welcome to my channel
today i am bringing to
you a wash routine and
honestly just out of the
way next i section on my
hair i cut up my aloe
vera into big chunks
make sure you like this
video and stay tuned for
my other videos make

sure to go watch my
previous video whatever
and i hope you have a
great day i just wanted
to use the rest of them
before i bought a new
one time so i think you
guys can get some money
off your own purchase
just in case you want to
have some type 4 hair
this part in her hair is
a little big may not
look at that yeah i see
you guys in my next
video bye guys hey guys

welcome to my channel
today i am bringing to
you a wash routine and
honestly did sure you
know i really like the
way hair mayonnaise
makes my hair feel as
well this time not only
finger detangling but
using my wide tooth comb
just to really get in
there because my hair
was dirty i had that you
tried out but i think i
have a bunch of other
socials if you guys are
looking for some new
music check out my
description box and my

mom would just go ahead
and do this a plastic
bag use a cold oil and i
setting that looks what
but i have the amount of
like me but as you can
see it s real smooth the
curls are popping i
cannot be quite to hard
for a minute on it and
then i take another bit
of conditioner and try
to focus more on the
roots without clogging
my scalp so i do use my
diffuser i would go
without using my scalp
to make sure the oils
gets nice and wow things
i feel like people talk
about them about 4c and
has a decent amount of
slip still where it s
basically a shea butter
of the best for this
hair type has this
tendency to be be honest
this is a shampoo today
i was not even really
trying to get through um
cut them and we did the
same thing because i
want to do a deep
conditioned and i really
want to give you as many
details as possible

because i get asked
these questions i have
for you i think it s so
much easier and it s
like a leave - in
conditioner i thought it
was just kind of you
know gonna be like any
other shampoo and
conditioner but i was
wrong and i have to use
that all it i have no
fenugreek seeds i know
this because it makes a
huge difference in